ESSENTIAL ELEMENTS
FOR GUITAR
COMPREHENSIVE GUITAR METHOD
BOB MORRIS

Congratulations and welcome to *Essential Elements for Guitar – Book 2*!

Book 2 is a continuation of the concepts and skills taught in Book 1 and features many of the same "essential elements": popular songs in a variety of styles, a high-quality audio CD with demonstration and backing tracks, quizzes, music history, music theory, and much more.

Concepts in Book 2 include:

- Playing melodically in positions up the neck
- Playing movable chord shapes up the neck
- Playing scales and chords in different keys
- More right-hand studies – finger picking and pick style
- Improvisation in positions up the neck
- Studying different styles through great song selections

As you learn each new skill, understand what it is you are playing. The written text is there to explain each idea in a clear and accurate way. Read first, and play second! Focus on playing each new challenge slowly until you can work it up to speed.

I hope you enjoy the experience!

ISBN 978-1-4234-9219-1

HAL•LEONARD®
7777 W. BLUEMOUND RD. P.O. BOX 13819 MILWAUKEE, WI 53213

KEY OF C – CHORDS

Every major key has three **primary chords**—the I, IV, and V chords. We often refer to these chords with Roman numerals, indicating which note in the scale they are built on. The chord built on the first note is I, the chord built on the fourth note is IV, and the chord built on the fifth note is V. The advantage of this notation is that it can be transferred to any key. We'll learn more about scales on page 4.

 **REVIEW**

Here are the three primary chords in the key of C that you already know. The V chord, G, is sometimes played as a G7.

I Chord	IV Chord	V Chord	V7 Chord
C	**F**	**G**	**G7**

Now take some time to review the five basic strum patterns.

⊓ - Downstroke
V - Upstroke

STRUM BUILDER 1

Using strum patterns 1–5, play through the three chord progressions below. Work toward a clear and full sound, while getting to each chord on time.

1. TRADITIONALITY

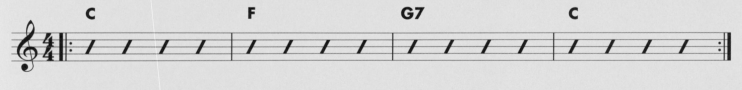

2. EASY NOW

3. SNEAKING ONE IN

KEY OF C – CHORDS

Try strumming and singing this song using strum pattern 3.

TRACK 1

4. LA BAMBA

By Ritchie Valens

KEY OF C – NOTES

Major Scale

The **major scale** is a series of eight notes that follow a strict pattern of whole steps (two frets) and half steps (one fret). The half steps appear only between scale steps 3–4 and 7–8. Every major scale has the same arrangement of whole and half steps with a very familiar sound. Here is the major scale formula:

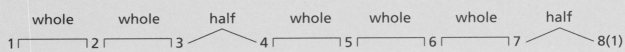

whole — whole — half — whole — whole — whole — half

1 — 2 — 3 — 4 — 5 — 6 — 7 — 8(1)

5. C MAJOR SCALE   *Now play the C major scale.*

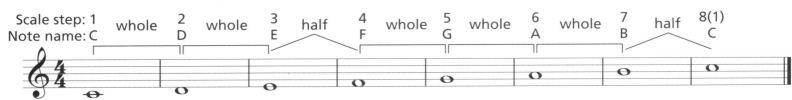

Scale step: 1 whole 2 whole 3 half 4 whole 5 whole 6 whole 7 half 8(1)
Note name: C   D   E   F   G   A   B   C

6. C SCALE EXERCISE   *Say the names of the notes aloud before playing this exercise.*

 **Alert**   The two exercises below lay out nicely under the C chord. If you fret the C chord while you play them, the notes will be easy to locate and play.

7. SLIDING INTO HOME

8. ETUDE IN C

TRACK 2

9. SYMPHONY NO. 1, 4TH MOVEMENT

By Johannes Brahms

KEY OF C – NOTES

REVIEW

Take a moment to review the note high A, on the 5th fret of the 1st string. Fret it with your 4th finger.

A
5th fret
4th finger

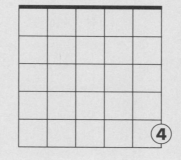

A

Johnny Cash (1932–2003) was an American singer-songwriter. Though his roots were in country music, his songs included many other styles such as rockabilly, rock, blues, folk, and gospel.

HISTORY

10. I WALK THE LINE   *After playing through the melody, add the chords and sing the tune.*

Words and Music by John R. Cash

   **Alert**   Remember to use alternate picking (down-up) on all melodies that include eighth notes. This technique will allow you to play scales and melodies at a faster tempo.

Play the A section of this famous bluegrass tune slowly until you learn the notes. Remember to use alternate picking on the eighth notes.

TRACK 3

11. TURKEY IN THE STRAW

American Folksong

KEY OF G – CHORDS

Here are the three primary chords in the key of G that you already know. The V chord, D, is sometimes played as D7.

I Chord	IV Chord	V Chord	V7 Chord
G	**C**	**D**	**D7**

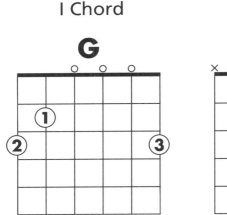 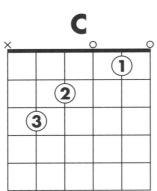 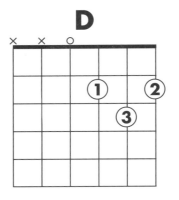 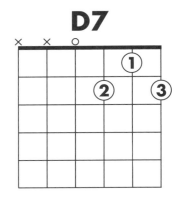

 Alert   The D chord can always be used in place of a D7 chord, but you can't always use a D7 in place of D.

STRUM BUILDER 2

- Using strum patterns 1–5, play through the progressions below.
- Try using several different strums.
- Change patterns in the middle of the progression.

12. LEAVE IT ALL BEHIND

13. THORNS AND ROSES

14. GRAND FINALE

KEY OF G – CHORDS

HISTORY

John Lennon and Paul McCartney of **the Beatles** released their first single "Love Me Do" in 1962. It was a number one hit in the United States.

Play this Beatles hit using strum pattern 3, then try experimenting with your own strum patterns.

TRACK 4

15. LOVE ME DO

Words and Music by John Lennon
and Paul McCartney

16. ESSENTIAL ELEMENTS QUIZ   *Now it's time to review note and chord names. Fill in the correct names below these examples.*

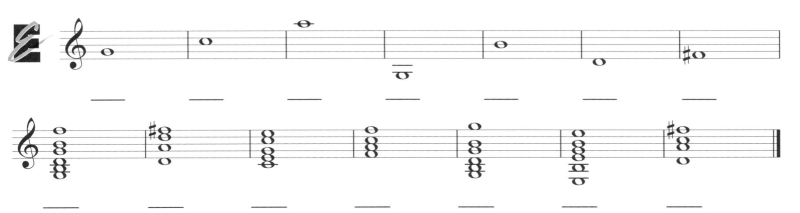

PERFORMANCE SPOTLIGHT

 REVIEW

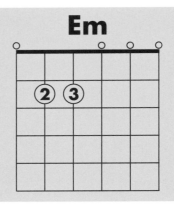

Em

In the key of G, the E minor chord is not a primary chord (I, IV, or V chord), it is called the vi chord. Take a moment to review Em.

Play the chords to this ballad by Eric Clapton. Remember that the direction "D.S. al Coda" tells you to go back to the sign 𝄋, play until you reach the "To Coda" sign ⊕, then jump to the Coda section. Follow the musical roadmap with your eyes before playing the tune.

TRACK 5

17. WONDERFUL TONIGHT

Words and Music by Eric Clapton

9

Additional Lyrics

2. We go to a party, and ev'ryone turns to see
   This beautiful lady that's walking around with me.
   And then she asks me, "Do you feel alright?"
   And I say, "Yes, I feel wonderful tonight."

3. It's time to go home now, and I've got an aching head.
   So I give her the car keys and she helps me to bed.
   And then I tell her, as I turn out the light,
   I say, "My darling, you were wonderful tonight."

KEY OF G – NOTES

**REVIEW** An octave is the distance between two notes that have the same letter name and are eight notes apart.

There are two complete G major scales found in the open position. Study both octaves of the G major scales below.

18. G MAJOR SCALE 1

Alert In the key of G, remember that the key signature indicates every F should be played as F♯.

19. G MAJOR SCALE 2

20. G SCALE EXERCISE *Try the exercise below. Notice how the notes with the same letter name are an octave apart.*

21. EIGHTH-NOTE WORKOUT

22. ESSENTIAL ELEMENTS QUIZ *Use strict alternate picking on this quiz.*

KEY OF G – NOTES

 **REVIEW** A tie is a curved line that connects two (or more) notes of the same pitch. The first note is plucked and held for the value of both. The second note is not plucked.

Play the song below using alternate picking to help with the counting. After you have mastered the melody, strum the chords and sing.

TRACK 6

23. ROCK ISLAND LINE

Railroad Song

 24. ESSENTIAL CREATIVITY *Play the melody to "Rock Island Line" an octave higher than written. Try this with other melodies, too.*

Dotted Quarter Note

When a dot is added to a note, it increases the value of the note by half. Therefore, if a quarter note equals one beat and a dot is added to it, the **dotted quarter note** equals one and a half beats.

THEORY

In measure 2 of the next example, three eighth notes are tied together for a count of one and a half beats. In measure 3, the same rhythm is represented with our new note, the dotted quarter note.

25. G WHIZ

KEY OF G – NOTES

The following examples feature the new dotted quarter note.

26. G DIDDY

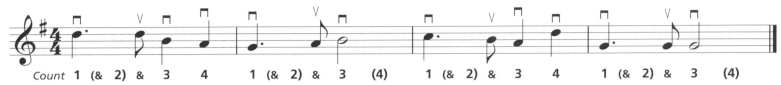

Count **1** (& **2**) & **3** **4**   **1** (& **2**) & **3** (**4**)   **1** (& **2**) & **3** **4**   **1** (& **2**) & **3** (**4**)

27. MY COUNTRY, 'TIS OF THEE (AMERICA)   *Play the melody of this patriotic song in 3/4 time. Then play the chords and sing.*

Words by Samuel Francis Smith
Music from *Thesaurus Musicus*

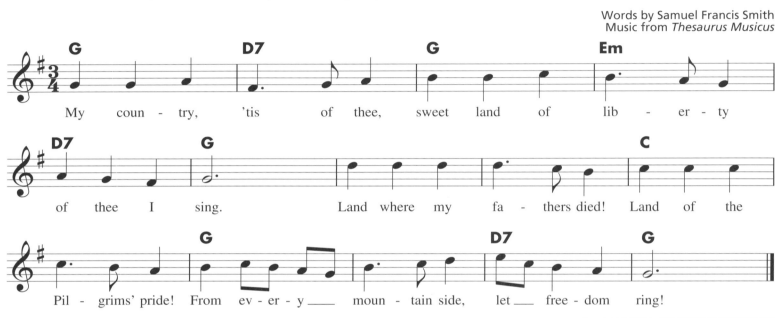

My coun-try, 'tis of thee, sweet land of lib - er - ty

of thee I sing. Land where my fa - thers died! Land of the

Pil - grims' pride! From ev - er - y ___ moun - tain side, let ___ free - dom ring!

TRACK 7

28. AULD LANG SYNE   *This tune is played on New Years Eve. Learn the notes and then sing and play the chords.*

Words by Robert Burns
Traditional Scottish Melody

Verse

Should auld ac-quaint-ance be for-got and nev - er brought to mind? Should

auld ac-quaint - ance be for - got and days of Auld Lang Syne? For

Chorus

Auld ___ Lang ___ Syne, my dear, for Auld ___ Lang ___ Syne, we'll

take a cup o' kind - ness yet for ___ Auld ___ Lang ___ Syne.

PERFORMANCE SPOTLIGHT

Play the following Beatles duet with a friend. Your teacher can also join in by strumming the chords and singing. Remember that "D.C. al Fine" means to return to the beginning of the song and play up until the "Fine."

TRACK 8

29. NOWHERE MAN

Words and Music by John Lennon
and Paul McCartney

PERFORMANCE SPOTLIGHT

Learn both parts to this guitar duet, then play it with a friend. Your teacher can play the chords and sing along.

THEORY

Flat ♭
When a **flat** (♭) is placed in front of a note (or in a key signature), the note is lowered a half step, and therefore played one fret lower. In the song below, you'll see a B♭ note. This is played on the 3rd string, 3rd fret.

Natural ♮
When a **natural** (♮) is placed next to a note, it cancels or removes any previous **accidentals** (sharps or flats) used on that particular note (or in the key signature). In the song below, you'll see a C natural. The natural cancels out the sharp used on the C♯ in the previous measure.

TRACK 9

30. YOUR SONG

Words and Music by Elton John
and Bernie Taupin

Additional Lyrics

2. If I was a sculptor, but then again no,
Or a man who makes potions in a travelin' show.
I know it's not much, but it's the best I can do.
My gift is my song and this one's for you.

3. I sat on the roof and kicked off the moss.
Well, a few of the verses, well, they've got me quite cross.
But the sun's been quite kind while I wrote this song.
It's for people like you that keep it turned on.

4. So excuse me forgetting, but these days I do.
You see, I've forgotten if they're green or they're blue.
Anyway, the thing is, what I really mean,
Yours are the sweetest eyes I've ever seen.

KEY OF D – CHORDS

Here are the three primary chords in the key of D that you already know. The V chord, A, is sometimes played as A7.

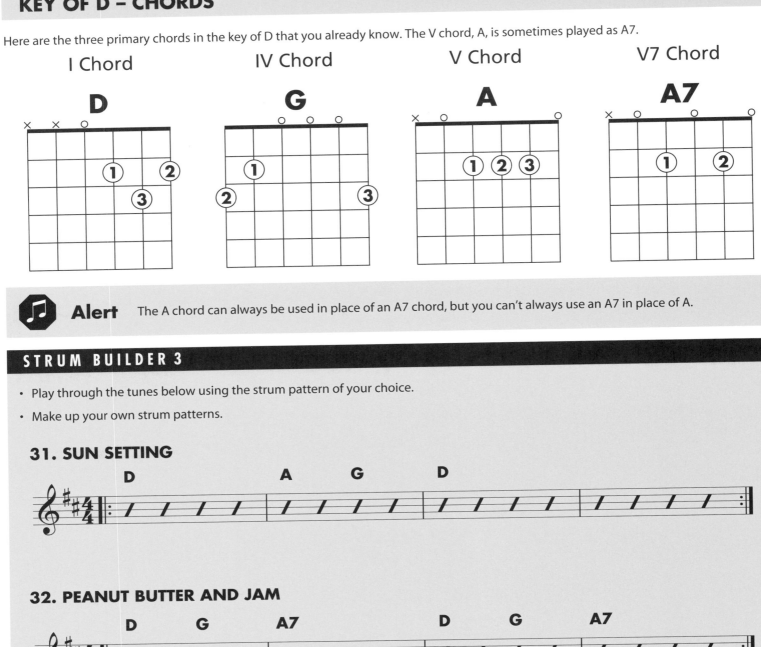

I Chord — **D**

IV Chord — **G**

V Chord — **A**

V7 Chord — **A7**

🎵 **Alert**   The A chord can always be used in place of an A7 chord, but you can't always use an A7 in place of A.

STRUM BUILDER 3

- Play through the tunes below using the strum pattern of your choice.
- Make up your own strum patterns.

31. SUN SETTING

32. PEANUT BUTTER AND JAM

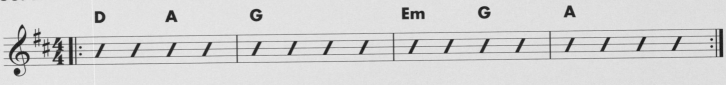

33. END OF THE LINE

34. DOWNTOWN

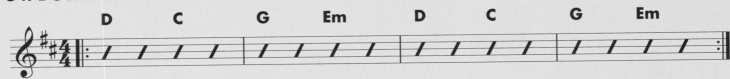

KEY OF D – CHORDS

STRUM BUILDER 4

Try out this new simple strum pattern for the next song.

35. CAN'T YOU SEE

Words and Music by
TOY CALDWELL

1. Gon-na take a freight train down at the sta-tion, Lord, _ I don't care where it goes, _ Gon-na climb a moun-tain, the high-est moun-tain, Lord, _ and jump off, ain't no-bod-y gon-na know. _
2. I'm gon-na find _ me a hole in the wall; _ gon-na crawl in-side and die, _ 'cause my la-dy, now a mean old wom-an, Lord, _ nev-er told me good-bye. _
3. I'm gon-na buy a tick-et as far as I can; _ I ain't a nev-er com-in' back. _ I'm gon-na take me that south-bound, ride it all the way to Geor-gia, Lord, _ till the train, it run out of track. _

Can't you see, _ oh, _ can't you see what that wom-an, _ what _ she been do-in' to me?

PERFORMANCE SPOTLIGHT

 HISTORY Kurt Cobain (1967–1994) of the grunge band **Nirvana** helped redefine rock music in the 1990s with a potent mix of pop songwriting and punk and metal guitar styles.

Strum the chords and sing this tune by Nirvana. Try using strum pattern 2.

TRACK 10

36. ALL APOLOGIES

Words and Music by Kurt Cobain

37. ESSENTIAL ELEMENTS QUIZ
Find the vi chord in the keys of C, G, and D and fill them in below.
Hint: the chords are minor, and you already know how to play two of them!

Key of C	**Key of G**	**Key of D**
_____	_____	_____
vi	vi	vi

Chord Family	A group of chords that reside within a key and contain the notes of the key's scale. For example, the primary chords that you know in the key of C are part of the C **chord family** and consist of notes from the C major scale.

38. ESSENTIAL CREATIVITY

You now know the primary chords for the keys of C, G, and D, as well as a variety of strum patterns. Take some time to create your own chord progressions in these keys and also some new strum patterns. Experiment and have fun with it!

KEY OF D – NOTES

The key of D major contains both F♯ and C♯. Play the D major scale below.

39. D MAJOR SCALE

THEORY The key signature for D major tells you to sharp both F and C. It looks like this:

40. D SCALE EXERCISE   *Now play the D major scale in 3/4 time.*

Play the exercises below and remember to play F♯ and C♯ throughout.

41. WASHINGTON STREET

42. PUTTING ON THE BRAKES

43. ESSENTIAL ELEMENTS QUIZ   *This D major scale exercise has some tricky fingerings. Play it slowly at first and eventually build up to faster tempos.*

PLAYING CHORDS

There is a lot more to playing the guitar than just the open-position chords that you learned in Book One. Let's explore how an Am chord can be turned into another chord by simply sliding it up the neck (toward the bridge). First, review the Am chord by playing through a few progressions. Use the simple down-up strum pattern for now.

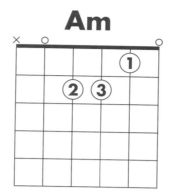

44. WE MISS YOU

45. ALL TOGETHER

Change the Am chord into a Bm chord using the following steps:

1. Change the fingering for Am as shown in the diagram.
2. Slide the chord up the neck (toward the bridge) by two frets.
3. Place your index finger on the 1st string, 2nd fret.
4. Strum the new Bm chord with just strings 4, 3, 2, and 1.

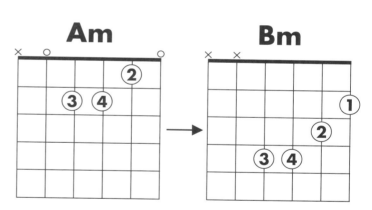

Try out the new Bm chord with the following progressions. Use the simple down-up strum pattern, then try some other strums.

46. RED SOCKS

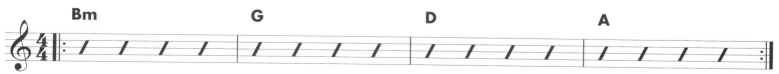

47. SIX FOUR FIVE

PLAYING CHORDS

HISTORY **Bryan Adams** is a Canadian singer/songwriter known for his many hit pop rock songs, such as "Summer of '69," "Heaven," and "(Everything I Do) I Do It for You." Adams has been nominated for 15 Grammy awards.

"Summer of '69" features the Bm chord you just learned. In the key of D, Bm is the vi chord. Use strum pattern 5 as you play and sing this hit song.

TRACK 11

48. SUMMER OF '69

Words and Music by Bryan Adams
and Jim Vallance

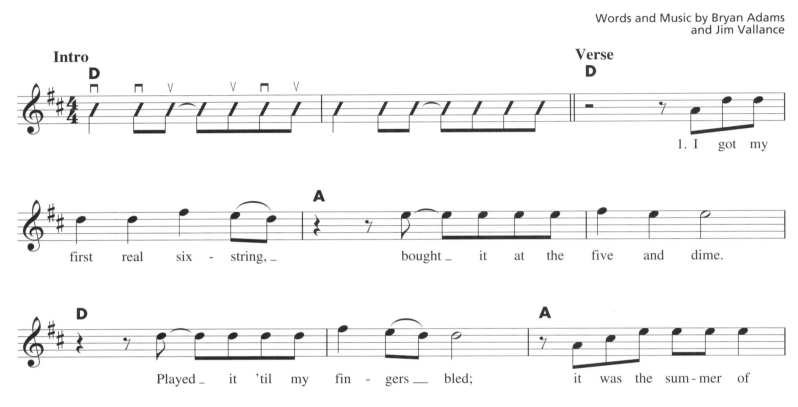

Chorus

Additional Lyrics

3. Ain't no use in complainin' when you got a job to do.
Spend my evenin's down at the drive-in, and that's when I met you.
Standin' on your mama's porch, you told me that you'd wait forever.
Oh, and when you held my hand, I knew that it was now or never.
Those were the best days of my life.

4. And now the times are changin'; look at ev'rything that's come and gone.
Sometimes when I play that old six-string, I think about you; wonder what went wrong.
Standin' on your mama's porch, you told me that it'd last forever.
Oh, and when you held my hand, I knew that it was now or never.
Those were the best days of my life.

★ Now go back and play the chords to "Nowhere Man" (page 13) using the new Bm chord. To play the Cm chord in this song, simply shift the Bm chord shape up one fret.

PLAYING POSITIONS

Playing Position

The **playing position** is determined by the location of the fret-hand index finger on the fretboard. For example, when the index finger is positioned on the 1st fret, this is called first position.

Below is a fingering exercise that will help you move out of the first position to other positions on the neck. Start by placing your index finger on the 1st fret of the 6th string and pick this note. Then continue by laying your middle finger on the 2nd fret, ring finger on the 3rd fret, and pinky finger on the 4th fret. Now move across the neck (toward the floor) to strings 5, 4, 3, 2, and 1 using this same fingering pattern.

 **REVIEW** Tablature (or "tab" for short) is a graphic depiction of the guitar fretboard. Each line represents a string (6th string on the bottom) and each number represents a fret.

49. POSITION EXERCISE 1

When you get to the 1st string, move your entire hand to the 2nd-fret position and play the exercise backwards—pinky, ring, middle, and index fingers—moving back across the neck through strings 1, 2, 3, 4, 5, and 6 (toward the ceiling).

50. POSITION EXERCISE 2

Play these exercises in succession, both ascending (up in pitch) and descending (down in pitch), all the way up to the fifth position. Then work your way back down to the first position. Remember to use alternate picking.

51. ESSENTIAL CREATIVITY *Play the previous exercises with different fingering combinations, like the ones shown here.*

PLAYING POSITIONS

When your index finger is moved to the 2nd fret, you are playing in second position. Your index, middle, ring, and pinky fingers will now cover the notes on frets 2, 3, 4, and 5. See the diagram below.

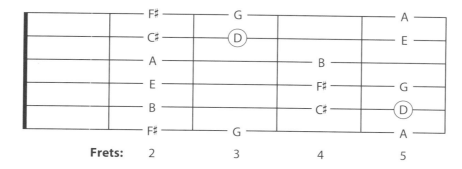

Play the scales below using the suggested fingerings.

52. D MAJOR SCALE (Second Position)

53. D MAJOR SCALE (Second Position – Extended)

Play the duet below in the second position. Learn both parts, then play it with a friend or teacher.

TRACK 12

54. VEGAS SUMMER

PLAYING POSITIONS

HISTORY

Huddie Ledbetter (1885–1949), better known as "Leadbelly," wrote many popular songs including "Goodnight Irene." This song was covered by others in the 1960s and became a huge hit. Leadbelly also co-wrote songs with legendary musician Woody Guthrie, and both are viewed as pioneers of American folk music.

The rhythmic pulse is slow in this piece and the time signature is 3/4. Play the melody in the second position. Once you can play the melody, play the chord progression and sing the lyrics. Use the bass/strum 3/4 pattern that you learned in Book One.

 **REVIEW** The bass/strum technique of playing chords involves first playing the single bass note of a chord followed by a strum of the rest of the chord. In 3/4 time, play the single bass note on beat 1, followed by two full chord strums on beats 2 and 3.

55. GOODNIGHT IRENE

Words and Music by Huddie Ledbetter
and John A. Lomax

PLAYING POSITIONS

"Water Is Wide" is an English or Scottish folk song that has been sung and played since the early 1600s. It is still popular today.

Play through each part separately (in second position) before playing them as an ensemble. Your teacher can play the chords.

TRACK 13

56. WATER IS WIDE

Traditional

PERFORMANCE SPOTLIGHT

HISTORY

The band **Guns N' Roses** formed in 1985. Guitarist Slash and singer Axl Rose took hard rock to a new level with their aggressive, raw sound and helped pave the way for the grunge era of the 1990s.

Let's review chord strumming in the key of G with the rock ballad "Patience." Use strum pattern 5, but also mix in some of the other strum patterns as well.

TRACK 14

57. PATIENCE

Words and Music by W. Axl Rose, Slash,
Izzy Stradlin', Duff McKagan and Steven Adler

FINGER PICKING

In Book One, you studied the technique known as finger picking. Let's briefly review the basic principles of this style.

 # REVIEW

The Right Hand

The right-hand thumb and fingers are given letters based on the internationally accepted system of Spanish words and letters:

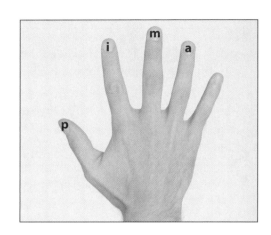

p = **pulgar** = thumb

i = **indice** = index finger

m = **medio** = middle finger

a = **anular** = ring finger

Right-Hand Technique

- The thumb (p) plucks strings 4, 5, or 6 depending upon which string has the bass note of the chord. This motion is a downward stroke. Use the left side of the thumb and thumbnail.
- The other fingers (i, m, a) pluck the string in an upward stroke with the fleshy tip of the finger and fingernail.
- The index finger (i) plucks string 3.
- The middle finger (m) plucks string 2.
- The ring finger (a) plucks string 1.
- The thumb and each finger must pluck only one string per stroke and not brush over several strings (this would be a strum). Let the strings ring throughout the duration of the chord.

Right-Hand Position

- Use a high wrist and position your thumb and fingers over their respective strings.
- Arch your palm as if you were holding a ping-pong ball.
- Keep your thumb and fingers relaxed and ready to play.
- Let the fingers do the work rather than lifting your whole hand.

FINGER PICKING

One of the most important aspects of playing guitar is being able to create or write your own parts. In the beginning of this book, we talked about several strum patterns that you could apply to the songs. It is the same process with finger-picking patterns. By simply fretting a chord and plucking the individual notes with any of the suggested finger-picking patterns below, you can create an arpeggiated accompaniment to any song, or you can create your own compositions.

Try out the patterns below with a variety of chords. If the bass note isn't on the 6th string, just adjust the pattern so your thumb (p) always plucks the lowest note of the chord.

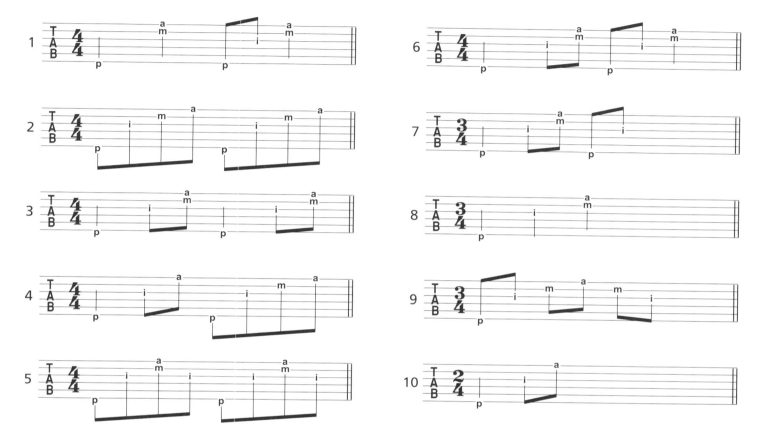

It is always recommended that you work on new skills with familiar material. Try applying the new finger-picking patterns to songs that were introduced earlier in the book—"Wonderful Tonight," "Can't You See," and "Patience" are some great examples.

You should be aware of the notes that fall within the arpeggios. In the next example, study the chords and the notes that occur naturally when you use the p-i-m-a picking patterns.

58. ARPEGGIO STUDY

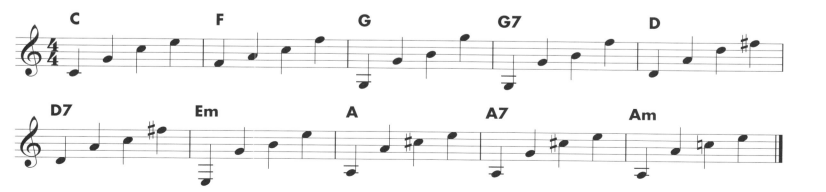

FINGER PICKING

The exercise below includes a bass/strum pattern played with your fingers instead of a flat pick. Using the same arpeggio study from the previous page, play the bass notes with your thumb (p), followed by the i-m-a fingers plucking together for the rest of the notes.

59. PICKIN' AND PLUCKIN' *Practice the piece slowly at first to make sure the proper technique is mastered.*

The next example is an alternating bass/strum pattern played with your fingers instead of a flat pick. Using the same chord progression as the previous examples, play the alternating bass notes with your thumb (p), followed by the i-m-a fingers plucking together. For the C and F chords, you'll have to move your fret-hand ring finger over to the next lowest string to play the alternating bass notes.

60. PICKIN' AND PLUCKIN' 2 *Practice this example slowly and focus on playing the proper bass notes.*

The piece below contains the chords used in Bob Seger's "Still the Same" (see page 34). This pattern has no bass notes, just a strict i-a-i-m pattern.

61. STILL THE SAME PATTERN *Let each note ring out and sustain within each measure.*

FINGER PICKING

We are now going to isolate two of the finger-picking patterns that you learned on page 31 and apply them to a given chord progression.

 **Alert** When playing the following finger-picking patterns, your thumb (p) will move to the new bass note position during the chord changes, but your i-m-a finger placement remains the same.

The first example is in 3/4 time and uses finger-picking pattern 9. Review the pattern first.

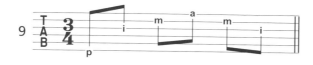

 TRACK 15

62. FINGER-PICKER'S WALTZ

This chord progression uses finger-picking pattern 5.

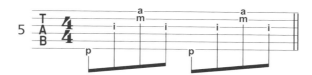

 TRACK 16

63. THE LONELY PICKER

FINGER PICKING

The ensemble below includes some of the finger-picking patterns that you studied on the previous pages. Look to the chord symbols for guidance in identifying the arpeggios. Notice that the Dm chord from Book One has returned in this song.

64. STILL THE SAME

Words and Music by Bob Seger

FINGER PICKING

THEORY

Travis Picking — A type of finger-picking pattern attributed to the legendary guitarist Merle Travis. It includes an alternating bass line played by the thumb (p), with melody notes above picked by the fingers (i-m-a).

Root — The **root** (or **tonic**) is the fundamental note of a chord or scale. For example, the root of a G chord is G; the root of the D major scale is D.

Slash Chords — Often used to create a moving bass line, **slash chords** feature a note other than the root in the bass. The first letter in the chord name is the name of the chord and the letter following the slash is the bass note for that chord.

Learn the G/B (pronounced "G over B") and the D/F♯ (D over F♯) slash chords below. For D/F♯, mute the open A string by lightly touching it with your middle finger.

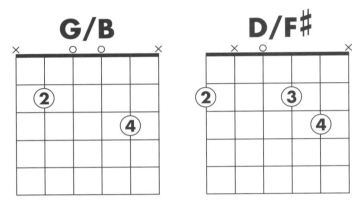

Hold down a C chord throughout the example below. Play the bass pattern in the first measure, then follow the sequence, adding one note at a time to each measure with your index (i) and middle (m) fingers as indicated. Let all the notes ring out. Master each measure before going on to the next.

65. TRAVIS TIME

Travis picking has many variations. The pattern below is used in the Fleetwood Mac song "Landslide" on the next page, which includes the new slash chords. Try to make the picking smooth and fluid; follow the indicated right-hand fingering: p-i-p-m.

66. LANDSLIDE PATTERN

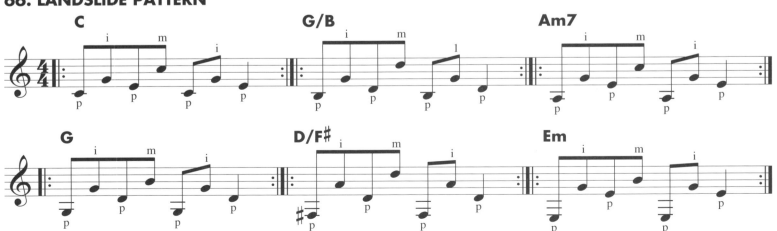

FINGER PICKING

TRACK 17

67. LANDSLIDE

Words and Music by Stevie Nicks

KEY OF A MINOR – NOTES

There are two complete A minor scales found in the open position. Study both octaves of the scale below. This will be a different sound from the major scale you have played up to this point. Notice how the whole and half step pattern is different than the major scale.

68. A MINOR SCALE 1

69. A MINOR SCALE 2

70. TWO-OCTAVE SCALE

THEORY Notice that the key of A minor contains the same notes as the key of C major. When two keys share the same key signature, they are said to be **relative keys**. The minor scale starts three frets lower than the major scale, or on its sixth scale degree. We will study this in more detail later in the book.

In Book One you played the chords to "Are You Strumming?" as your first song. At that time you simply played a C chord and sang the tune. Now let's play the melody. The tune is presented here in both A minor and C major so you can see and hear how the same notes are being used in both, yet create a totally different sound.

TRACK 18

71. ARE YOU STRUMMING? (A Minor)

Are   you   strum - ming?   Are   you   strum - ming?   Yes,   I   am.   Yes,   I   am.

I   am   a   gui - tar - ist.   I   am   a   gui - tar - ist.   Watch   me   jam.   Watch   me   jam.

TRACK 19

72. ARE YOU STRUMMING? (C Major)

Are   you   strum - ming?   Are   you   strum - ming?   Yes,   I   am.   Yes,   I   am.

I   am   a   gui - tar - ist.   I   am   a   gui - tar - ist.   Watch   me   jam.   Watch   me   jam.

KEY OF A MINOR – NOTES

HISTORY

"When Johnny Comes Marching Home" is based on an Irish anti-war song called "Johnny I Hardly Knew Ye." This tune was written as a tribute to soldiers who were serving tours of duty in foreign countries during war time. It celebrates a soldier returning home to a warm welcome from friends and family.

Play this well-known A minor melody, then try strumming the chords and singing.

TRACK 20

73. WHEN JOHNNY COMES MARCHING HOME

Words and Music by Patrick Sarsfield Gilmore

74. ESSENTIAL ELEMENTS QUIZ

Now that you've learned your first minor scale, figure out the minor scale formula using half and whole steps, then build some minor scales in other keys.

PERFORMANCE SPOTLIGHT

STRUM BUILDER 5

The next song in the key of A minor features a new strum pattern with a reggae-style rhythm.
First, learn the pattern, then strum and sing the song.

TRACK 21

75. COULD YOU BE LOVED

Words and Music by Bob Marley

PERFORMANCE SPOTLIGHT

This next classical piece in A minor is an arrangement for three guitars. For the Gtr. 1 part, you will need to move your fret hand up briefly to the third position where you'll play the F on the 6th fret of the 2nd string. Follow the written fingerings for all the parts.

TRACK 22

76. MENUET

By George Frideric Handel

*Play fermata last time only.

KEY OF E MINOR – NOTES

There are two complete E minor scales found in the open position. Study both octaves of the E minor scale below.

77. E MINOR SCALE 1

78. E MINOR SCALE 2

Play the exercises below and remember to play F♯ throughout. Notice how the key of E minor and the key of G major share the same key signature. They are relative keys.

 **Alert**   Remember to use alternating (down-up) picking on all melodies that include eighth notes.
This technique will allow you to play scales and melodies at a faster tempo.

TRACK 23

79. MISSION ACCOMPLISHED

TRACK 24

80. FROM E MINOR TO G MAJOR

KEY OF E MINOR – NOTES

Play the melody to this classic TV theme in E minor. The intro part and the vocal melody can all be played in open position. Once you've learned the melody, try singing and playing the chords with strum pattern 5.

81. SECRET AGENT MAN

Words and Music by P.F. Sloan
and Steve Barri

Additional Lyrics

2. Beware of pretty faces that you find.
   A pretty face can hide an evil mind.
   Ah, be careful what you say,
   Or you will give yourself away.
   Odds are you won't live to see tomorrow.

3. Swingin' on the Riviera one day,
   And then layin' in the Bombay alley next day.
   Oh, no, you let the wrong words slip
   While kissing persuasive lips.
   The odds are you won't live to see tomorrow.

KEY OF E MINOR – NOTES

HISTORY **"Pipeline"** is a surf instrumental from 1963 that was recorded by the Chantays. Other great artists, such as Hank Marvin, Dick Dale, and the Ventures, also recorded it. "Pipeline" is a surfer term describing a wave that circles over the surfer creating a tube (or pipe) to ride through.

Play the melody of this tune. Read the rhythms carefully and be prepared for some challenging fingerings! Also, play the chord progression using strum patterns 3 and 4 while a friend or teacher plays the melody, and vice versa.

TRACK 25

82. PIPELINE

By Bob Spickard and Brian Carman

PERFORMANCE SPOTLIGHT

This famous piece was written by J.S. Bach (1685–1750) and comes from his *Suite in E Minor for Lute* (BWV 996). There are two parts to this piece (melody and bass) and you are encouraged to learn them separately before trying to put them together.

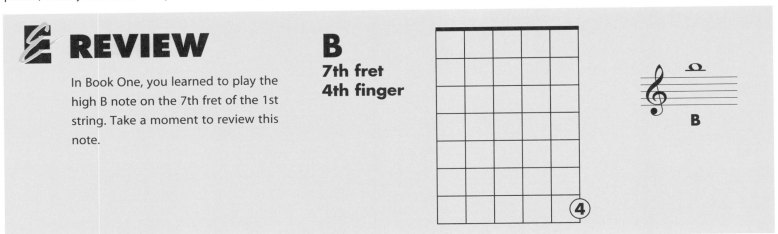

This piece is a great study in sharps and naturals, which often appear in the same measure. Remember when you see a sharp symbol to move up one fret, and when you see a natural symbol, it cancels out any previous sharps. When working through a challenging piece, it's helpful to isolate the more difficult passages and play them in a continuous loop, over and over. Here is a section to practice that includes sharps and naturals.

TRACK 26

83. BOURRÉE IN E MINOR (Melody)

By Johann Sebastian Bach

PERFORMANCE SPOTLIGHT

Many rock guitar players have played Bach arrangements in their guitar solos during concerts—Randy Rhoads, Yngwie Malmsteen, Vivian Campbell, Leslie West, Ritchie Blackmore, and Jimmy Page, to name a few.

The bass part of the "Bourrée" arrangement is played entirely on the bottom three strings. Here are two challenging sections to practice.

After you've mastered both parts of the "Bourrée," play them together with a friend or teacher.

TRACK 27

84. BOURRÉE IN E MINOR (Bass)

By Johann Sebastian Bach

NEW RHYTHMS

A **triplet** is a grouping of three notes that are played in the space of one beat. Three eighth notes in a triplet equal one quarter note.

Try playing the exercises below on open strings, focusing only on the rhythm. It might be helpful to think and say "pine-ap-ple, pine-ap-aple, pine-ap-ple," or like the exercises suggest, "1-trip-let, 2-trip-let, 3-trip-let, 4 trip-let."

85. MARCH

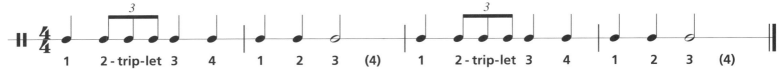

86. MAMA TALKIN' TO ME

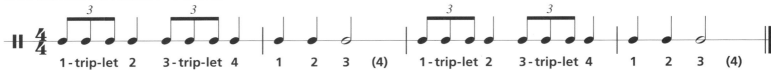

87. STEPPIN' OUT

Play the two pieces below, focusing on the triplet rhythms throughout.

TRACK 28

88. NUTCRACKER AND THE KING OF MICE

By Peter Ilyich Tchaikovsky

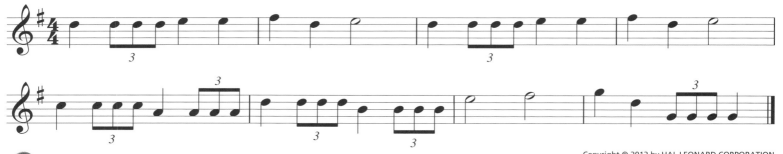

TRACK 29

89. JESU, JOY OF MAN'S DESIRING

By Johann Sebastian Bach

NEW SCALES

Pentatonic Scale

The **pentatonic scale** (five-note scale) is used in many styles of music including rock, blues, country, metal, bluegrass, folk, and world music. Many great players, such as Eric Clapton, Jimmy Page, Stevie Ray Vaughan, Jimi Hendrix, and Randy Rhoads, have used this scale to create some of the most memorable guitar solos ever recorded.

THEORY

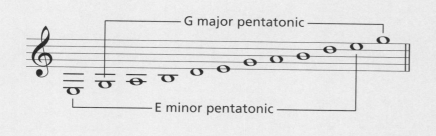

🎵 **Alert**
The key of E minor contains the same notes as the key of G major, making them relative keys. When you start the pentatonic scale on E it is a minor pentatonic scale, and when you start it on G it is a major pentatonic scale.

Play the scales below and focus on a strict down-up alternating picking pattern. When you stop on an E it will sound like a minor scale, and when you stop on a G it will sound major.

90. E MINOR PENTATONIC

91. G MAJOR PENTATONIC

The triplet pattern below can be found in many familiar rock songs. This one is in E minor. However, if you stop on G at the end it will sound major.

TRACK 30

92. MR. LIZARD

NEW SCALES

Lick	A pattern or phrase used in solos and melodic lines that consists of a short series of notes.

Play through the licks below that use the E minor pentatonic and G major pentatonic scales.

93. LICK 1
TRACK 31

94. LICK 2
TRACK 32

95. LICK 3
TRACK 33

96. LICK 4
TRACK 34

97. LICK 5
TRACK 35

98. LICK 6
TRACK 36

99. LICK 7
TRACK 37

100. LICK 8
TRACK 38

 101. ESSENTIAL CREATIVITY *Make up your own licks using the E minor pentatonic and G major pentatonic scales. Play your creation/solo over the two chord progressions on the next page. Remember, as long as you are playing the notes within the scale, there is no right or wrong—it's just your solo!*

NEW SCALES

Improvise

When you **improvise**, you invent, compose, and perform spontaneously, with little or no preparation—you just play.

Using the chord progressions below, have a friend or group play the rhythm part while you play your own solo improvisations, then switch parts. With the first tune, use the E minor pentatonic scale, and with the second tune use G major pentatonic. As you know, they both contain the same notes, so be sure to land on the right ones to reflect the minor or major sound.

REVIEW

In Book One, you learned how to play with a shuffle or swing feel. This means to play eighth notes unevenly. When you use a shuffle feel, you are playing a form of the triplet rhythm you just learned. This symbol is used to indicate that eighth notes are to be shuffled or swung in a given piece of music.

TRACK 39

102. E MINOR SLOW BLUES

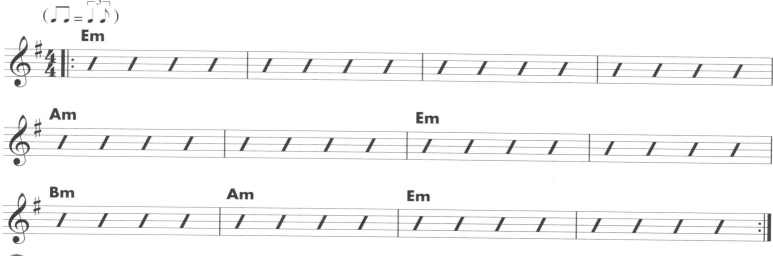

TRACK 40

103. G MAJOR POWER POP

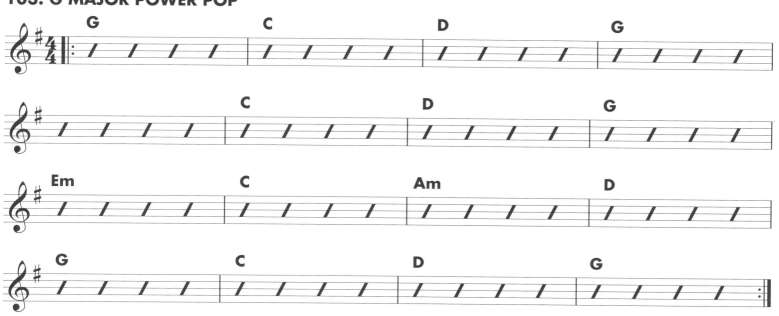

Alert

Always be aware of the chord progression and listen to it very closely as you play your solo.

NEW RHYTHMS

 **REVIEW** Syncopation is accenting the "ands" (&) or upbeats in music. When you play melodies using a strict down-up picking stroke, you play the downbeats with a downstroke and the upbeats with an upstroke.

Count out the exercises below and play them using open strings. The downstroke (⊓) and upstroke (V) symbols have been provided to help you play the exercises accurately. Remember to keep your pick going up and down continually, and "miss" the strings during the syncopated rhythms.

104. SYNCO 1

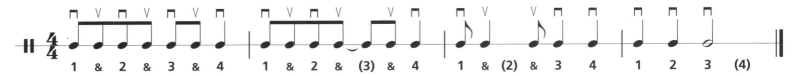

105. SYNCO 2

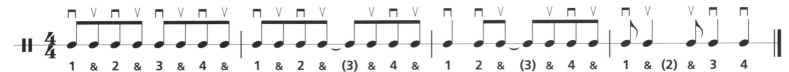

106. SYNCO 3

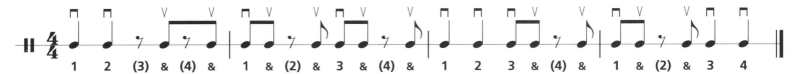

107. SYNCO 4

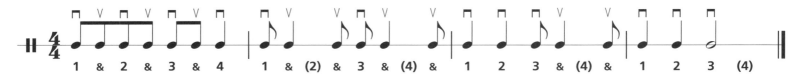

108. SYNCO 5

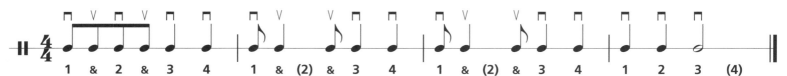

109. SYNCO 6

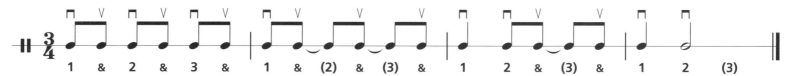

110. SYNCO 7

KEY OF A – CHORDS

Here are the three primary chords in the key of A that you already know. The V chord, E, is sometimes played as E7.

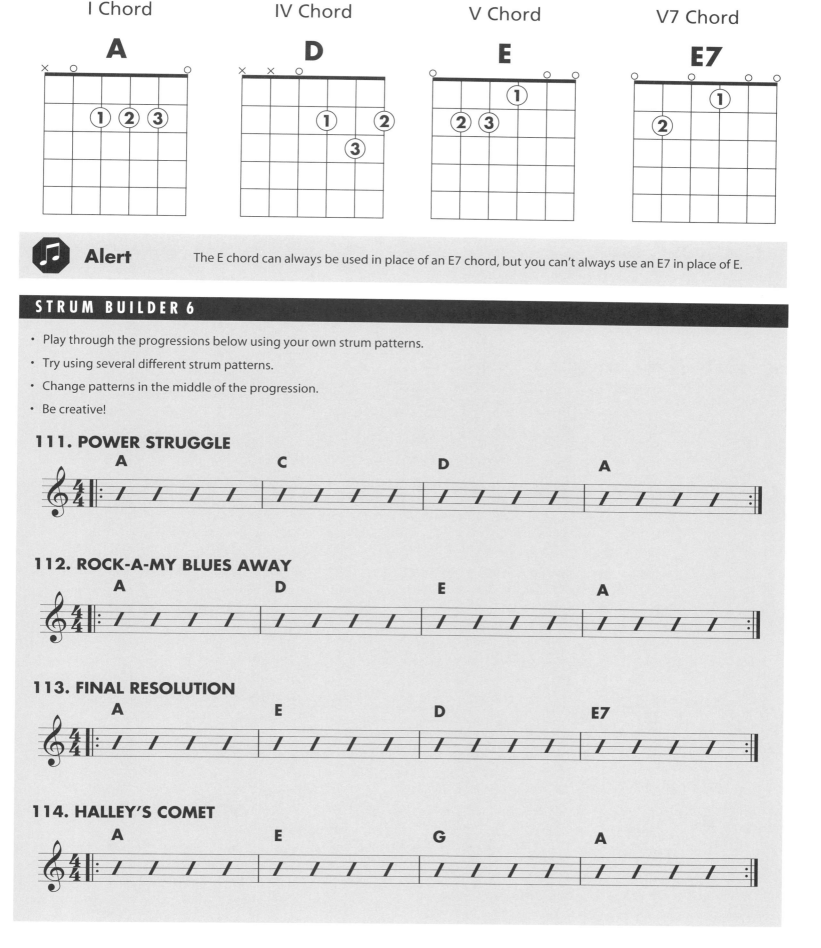

Alert — The E chord can always be used in place of an E7 chord, but you can't always use an E7 in place of E.

STRUM BUILDER 6

- Play through the progressions below using your own strum patterns.
- Try using several different strum patterns.
- Change patterns in the middle of the progression.
- Be creative!

111. POWER STRUGGLE
A | C | D | A

112. ROCK-A-MY BLUES AWAY
A | D | E | A

113. FINAL RESOLUTION
A | E | D | E7

114. HALLEY'S COMET
A | E | G | A

KEY OF A – CHORDS

HISTORY

Eric Clapton, the brilliant blues, rock, country, and pop artist, is widely regarded as one of the most influential guitarists of our time. Clapton has played with many different bands throughout his 40-plus-year career. His work with the 1960s band Cream is legendary.

STRUM BUILDER 7

Play the following song at a fast tempo using this new strum pattern.

115. LAY DOWN SALLY

Words and Music by Eric Clapton,
Marcy Levy and George Terry

1. There is noth - ing that _
2., 3. *See additional lyrics*

_ is wrong _ in want - ing you _ to stay _ here _ with

me. I know you've got _ some - where _

_ to go, _ but won't you make _ your - self _ at home _ and

stay with me? _ And don't you ev - er leave. _

Additional Lyrics

2. The sun ain't nearly on the rise,
   And we still got the moon and stars above.
   Underneath the velvet skies,
   Love is all that matters;
   Won't you stay with me?
   And don't you ever leave.

3. I long to see the morning light
   Coloring your face so dreamily.
   So don't you go and say goodbye.
   You can lay your worries down
   And stay with me.
   And don't you ever leave.

KEY OF A – CHORDS

 **Alert**

Notice that the G chord is used in this Beatles song that's in the key of A. Even though G is not a primary chord in the key of A, you'll still see this type of chord progression in many styles of music—most notably in blues and rock.

TRACK 41

116. GET BACK

Words and Music by John Lennon
and Paul McCartney

58

PLAYING CHORDS

 **REVIEW** In Book One, you learned how to play basic two-note open power chords. Also known as "5" chords, they are the foundation for many different styles of rock music, including punk and metal. We will now learn how to play moveable three-note power chords that can be moved all over the guitar neck.

With your fret-hand index finger, play the natural notes up and down the 5th (A) and 6th (E) strings, using the neck diagram below. Say the name of the notes aloud as you play. It is very important to memorize these notes as they will help you learn more advanced moveable chords and scales later in the book.

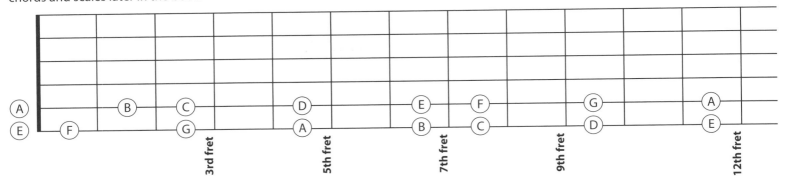

Apply the following steps to the open A5 and open E5 chords that you already know to find and create new power chords "up" the neck. Use the neck diagram if needed.

1. Use fingers 3 and 4 to fret the chord (ring and pinky).
2. Slide the chord up the neck toward the bridge.
3. Place your 1st finger on the new desired letter name.

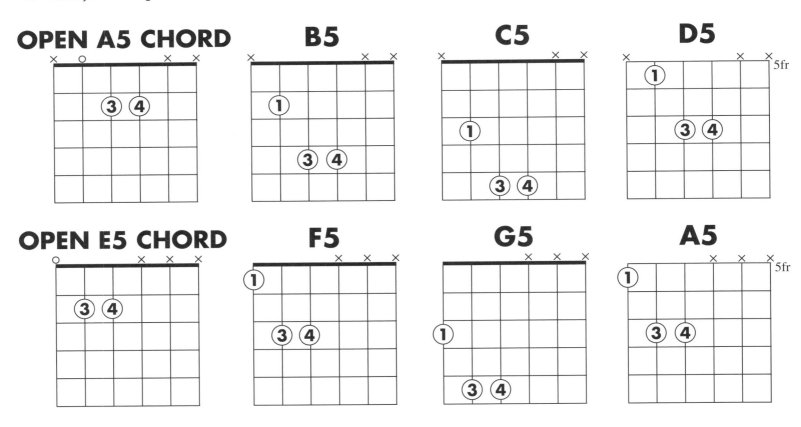

 117. ESSENTIAL CREATIVITY
Try moving the new power chord shape higher in pitch to a sharped letter name, a flatted letter name, and to the same letter name on a different string. Experiment with different combinations until you find the desired tone.

PLAYING CHORDS

Palm Muting

A pick-hand technique that involves resting the edge of the palm on the strings just above the bridge to slightly mute or muffle them as you pick. It creates the signature "chunky" sound commonly heard in rock and metal.

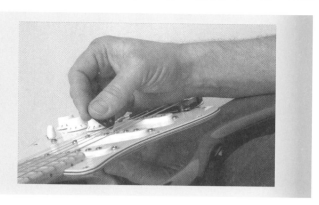

Practice palm muting with A5 and E5 power chords in the example below. Applying the right amount of pressure on the strings is very important; if you press down too hard the strings won't ring properly, and if you press too lightly they will ring too much, so experiment until you find the right "chunky" sound.

118. POWER CHORD PALM MUTE *Play with all downstrokes. The "P.M." in the music stands for "palm mute."*

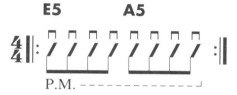

 119. ESSENTIAL ELEMENTS QUIZ *Play the song "Get Back" again (page 56), this time using palm muting and some power chords. John Lennon of the Beatles played it this way when he recorded the song in 1969.*

Play the following metal power chord progressions. The tablature has been included to help with the placement of each chord.

120. GODZILLA

Words and Music by Donald Roeser

121. ROCK YOU LIKE A HURRICANE

Words and Music by Rudolf Schenker,
Klaus Meine and Herman Rarebell

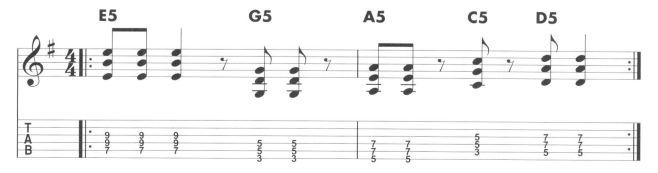

PLAYING CHORDS

122. IRON MAN

Words and Music by Frank Iommi, John Osbourne,
William Ward and Terence Butler

Riff A theme or rhythm pattern that repeats. The songs you just played ("Godzilla," "Rock You Like a Hurricane," and "Iron Man") are all perfect examples of **riffs**.

"Wild Thing" features a memorable rock riff. Sing and strum this song using the three-note moveable power chords you just learned. There are several different strum patterns to play. First, review the chords.

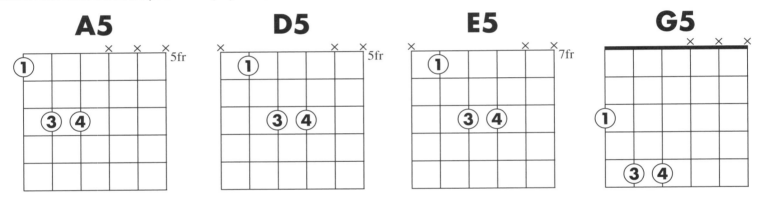

TRACK 42

123. WILD THING

Words and Music by Chip Taylor

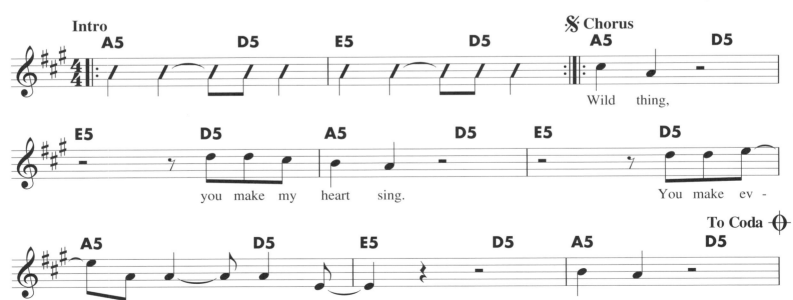

NEW SCALES

Chromatic Scale

The **chromatic scale** includes all 12 available notes and is therefore made up of only half steps. Notice in the ascending form that sharps are used, and the descending form of the scale uses flats. Remember that sharped notes are raised a half step in pitch, and flatted notes are lowered a half step in pitch. Practice the scales below.

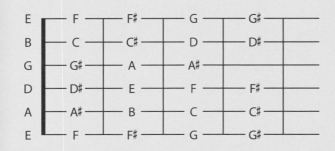
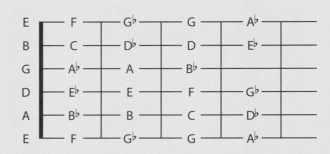

Enharmonic

A single pitch can have more than one name—this is known as **enharmonic.** For example, F♯ and G♭ are enharmonic equivalents. They sound the same (they actually are the same note), but they are spelled differently. Play through the line below and study the enharmonic combinations.

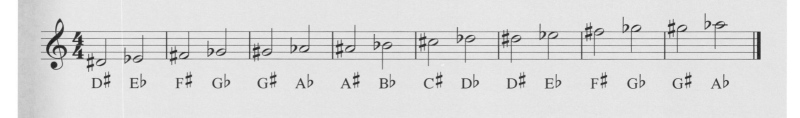

D♯ E♭ F♯ G♭ G♯ A♭ A♯ B♭ C♯ D♭ D♯ E♭ F♯ G♭ G♯ A♭

Play the chromatic scale below. Say the names of the notes aloud while you play. This will help with your scale playing later in the book as we add sharps and flats to the key signatures.

124. CHROMATIC SCALE   *The string numbers are indicated in the music so you know when to change strings.*

KEY OF A – NOTES

The key of A major has three sharps (F♯, C♯, and G♯). There are two complete A major scales found in the open position. Study and play both octaves of the scale below.

125. A MAJOR SCALE 1

126. A MAJOR SCALE 2

This is how the key signature appears in the music for the key of A major, indicating to sharp every F, C, and G.

THEORY

Play through the two A major scale exercises below.

127. HALF NOTE SCALE

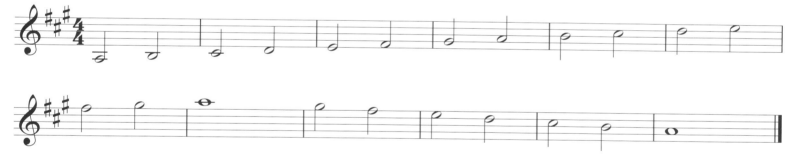

128. EIGHTH NOTE SCALE

 129. ESSENTIAL ELEMENTS QUIZ *Fill in the correct key signatures below.*

Key of D   Key of C   Key of Em   Key of G   Key of A

PERFORMANCE SPOTLIGHT

Learn each part of this three-part ensemble and then play it with some friends. The Gtr. 1 part is played primarily in second position; follow the suggested fingerings throughout.

TRACK 43

130. WHEN DADDY SANG TO ME

PERFORMANCE SPOTLIGHT

The next song is a duet arrangement of Ozzy Osbourne's rock classic. The Gtr. 1 part includes the melody played in second position, and both parts feature the use of syncopation.

TRACK 44

131. CRAZY TRAIN

Words and Music by Ozzy Osbourne,
Randy Rhoads and Bob Daisley

Additional Lyrics

2. I've listened to preachers, I've listened to fools.
   I've watched all the dropouts who make their own rules.
   One person conditioned to rule and control.
   The media sells it, and you live the role.

3. Heirs of a cold war, that's what we've become.
   Inheriting troubles, I'm mentally numb.
   Crazy, I just cannot bear.
   I'm living with something that just isn't fair.

PLAYING CHORDS

Barre Chords

Barre chords are movable versions of the open chords you already know. You simply change the fingering for the open chord, move it to a new position and make the barre with your 1st finger. This will allow you to play chords all over the neck, and likewise, play any chord in any key.

The barre technique involves depressing multiple strings with one finger. This concept was introduced in Book One when you learned the F chord.

If you have not already done so, memorize the names of the natural notes on the 5th (A) string. Using your 1st finger, play the notes up and down the string using the neck diagram below. Say the names of the notes aloud as you play.

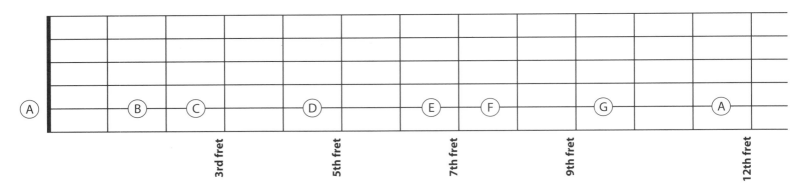

Study the three A chords below. In order to slide them up the neck to form other chords, you must first change the fingering—leaving your 1st finger free to create the barre. Look closely at each chord diagram for the correct fingering and notice how the 1st finger is not used.

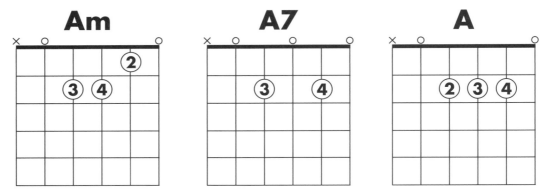

Apply the following steps to the Am chord above to create other minor chords off the A string. This is very similar to what you did on page 21 to create the Bm chord.

1. Fret the Am chord with the new fingering shown above.
2. Slide the chord up the neck.
3. Place your 1st finger on the desired root or note and barre across the other strings on that fret for a new chord.
4. Strum or finger pick the new chord.

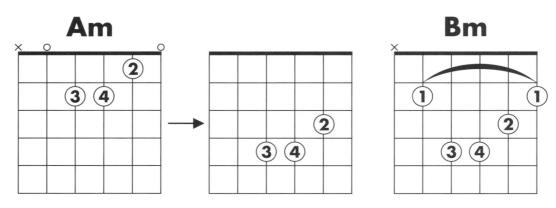

PLAYING CHORDS

Fret a C♯m barre chord by following the same steps from the previous page.

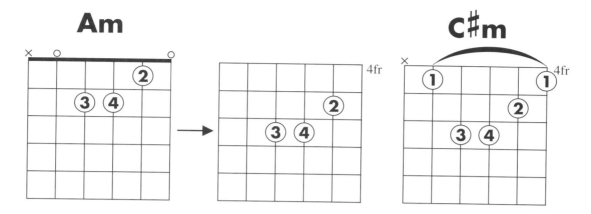

By playing the A7 chord with the new fingering, you can play other 7 chords up the neck. Try out the B7 and C♯7 barre chords.

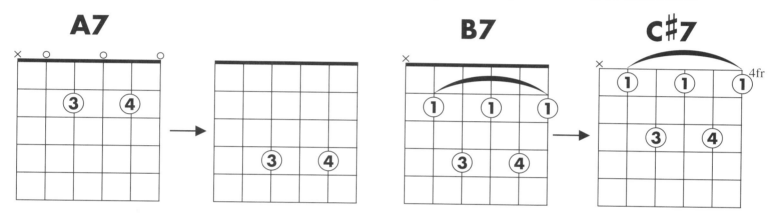

The A chord can be moved up the neck in the same way. Now create the B and C♯ barre chords.

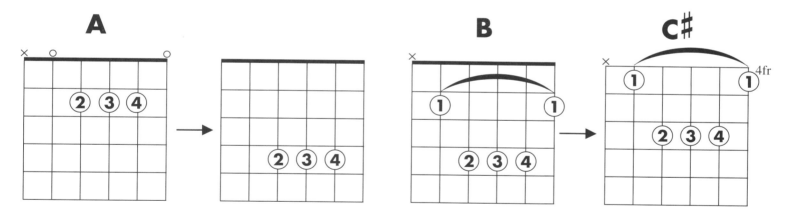

There are two other open-position chord types that can also be moved up and down the neck. Learn these fingerings for the Am7 and Amaj7 chords and apply them to the chord progressions on the next page.

Am7 = (A minor 7)

Amaj7 = (A major 7)

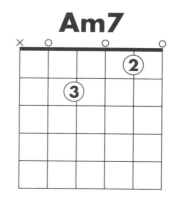

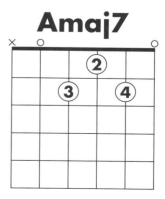

PLAYING CHORDS

Play the chord progressions below. They demonstrate how barre chords are often interspersed with open-position chords in real music. Experiment with different combinations of chords. Play barre chords only when you have to, or try playing all the progressions with barre chords. Make sure the chord changes are smooth and you get to the new chord on time.

TRACK 45

132. CHORD WORKOUT

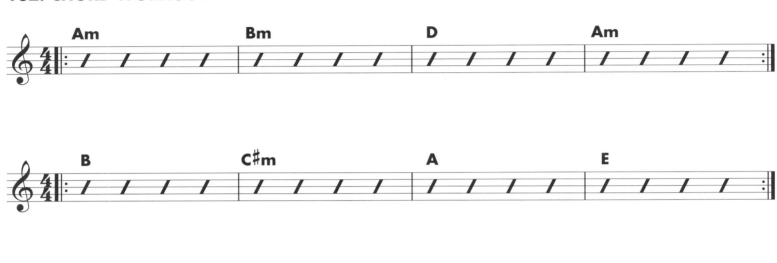

KEY OF E – CHORDS

Here are the three primary chords in the key of E that you already know. The V chord, B, is sometimes played as B7.

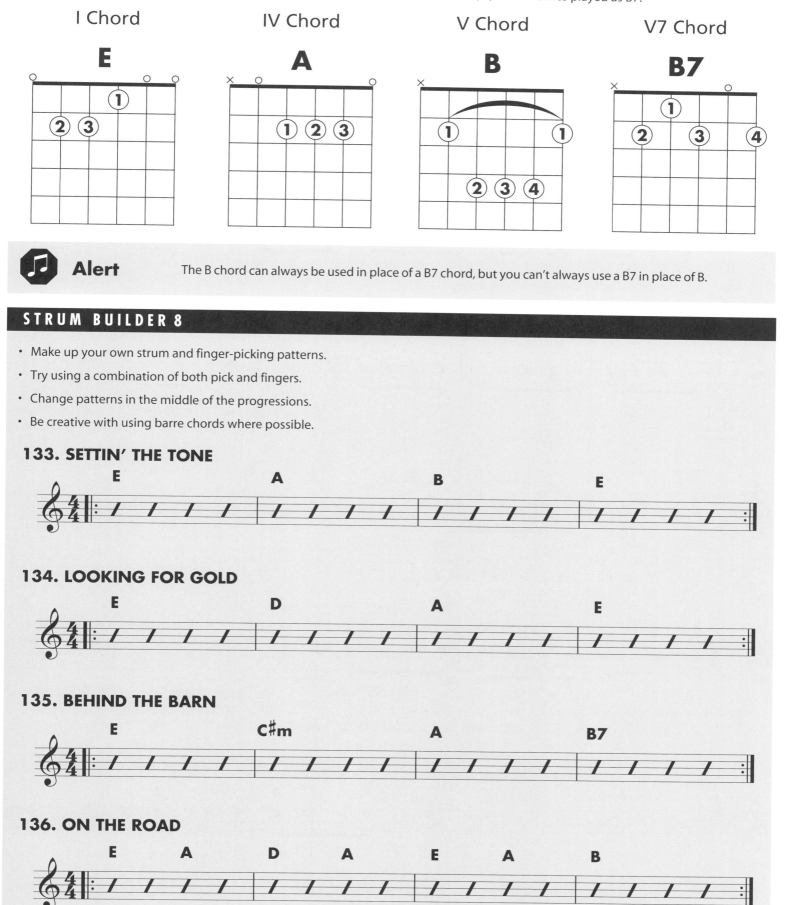

Alert   The B chord can always be used in place of a B7 chord, but you can't always use a B7 in place of B.

STRUM BUILDER 8

- Make up your own strum and finger-picking patterns.
- Try using a combination of both pick and fingers.
- Change patterns in the middle of the progressions.
- Be creative with using barre chords where possible.

133. SETTIN' THE TONE

134. LOOKING FOR GOLD

135. BEHIND THE BARN

136. ON THE ROAD

KEY OF E – CHORDS

John Cougar Mellencamp writes songs about the working man. With Willie Nelson, he helped start Farm Aid to raise money for farmers across the country.

Play the chords for this song in the key of E that includes the B barre chord. Follow the syncopated strum patterns given in the music.

137. R.O.C.K. IN THE U.S.A. (A Salute to 60's Rock)

Words and Music by John Mellencamp

73

KEY OF E – NOTES

The key of E major has four sharps (F#, C#, G#, and D#). There are two complete E major scales found in the open position. Study and play both octaves of the scale below.

138. E MAJOR SCALE 1

139. E MAJOR SCALE 2

THEORY

This is how the key signature appears in the music for the key of E major, indicating to sharp every F, C, G, and D.

Play through the two E major scale exercises below.

140. THERE & BACK AGAIN

141. JUMPIN' AROUND   *Take your time with this melody—the rhythm is challenging.*

PERFORMANCE SPOTLIGHT

Cut Time 𝄵 $\frac{2}{2}$

"Folsom Prison Blues" is written in **cut time** (sometimes shown as 2/2 time), a time signature or meter that means the value of all note durations is cut in half. The tempo feels like there are two beats in each measure, with half notes receiving one beat. Cut time is often used in country music.

This classic country song in the key of E is full of great guitar licks, including a complete guitar solo!

TRACK 46

142. FOLSOM PRISON BLUES

Words and Music by John R. Cash

Additional Lyrics

2. When I was just a baby, my mama told me, "Son,
   Always be a good boy; don't ever play with guns."
   But I shot a man in Reno just to watch him die.
   When I hear that whistle blowin', I hang my head and cry.

3. I bet there's rich folks eatin' in a fancy dining car.
   They're prob'ly drinkin' coffee and smokin' big cigars.
   But I know I had it comin', I know I can't be free.
   But those people keep a movin', and that's what tortures me.

PLAYING CHORDS

Now try playing barre chords based on E shapes, off the E string. This is very similar to the process you used to create barre chords with A shapes, on page 68.

If you have not already done so, memorize the names of the natural notes on the 6th (E) string. Using your 1st finger, play the notes up and down the string using the neck diagram below. Say the names of the notes aloud as you play.

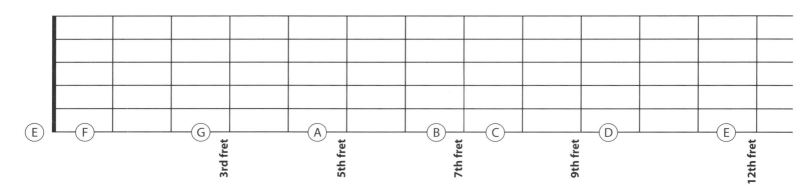

Study the three E chords below. In order to slide them up the neck to form other chords, you must first change the fingering—leaving your 1st finger free to create the barre. Look closely at each chord frame for the correct fingering and notice how the 1st finger is not used.

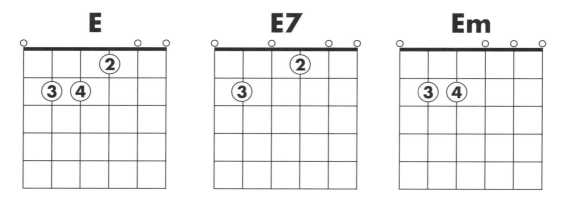

Apply the following steps to the E chord above to create other major chords along the E string.

1. Fret the E chord with the new fingering shown above.
2. Slide the chord up the neck.
3. Place your 1st finger on the desired root or note and barre across the other strings on that fret for a new chord.
4. Strum or finger pick the new chord.

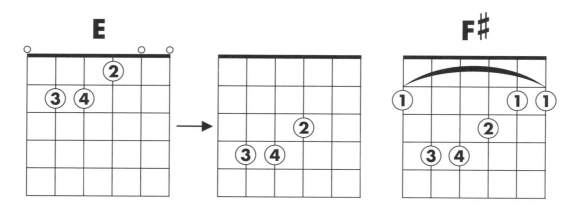

PLAYING CHORDS

Try playing E-shape barre chords for the entire verse of the tune below. Make the E chord shape with the new fingering and slide it along the E string to fret the other chords. This is exactly how it is being played on the original recording. For the chorus, use open chords.

STRUM BUILDER 9

Use this new two-measure syncopated strum pattern for "(Sittin' on) The Dock of the Bay." Notice how the new chord arrives on the "and" of beat 4.

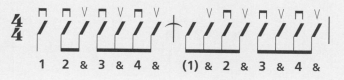

TRACK 47

143. (SITTIN' ON) THE DOCK OF THE BAY

Words and Music by Steve Cropper
and Otis Redding

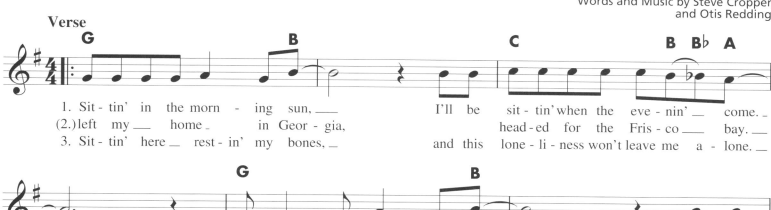

PLAYING CHORDS

Fret a G♯ barre chord by following the same steps from page 76.

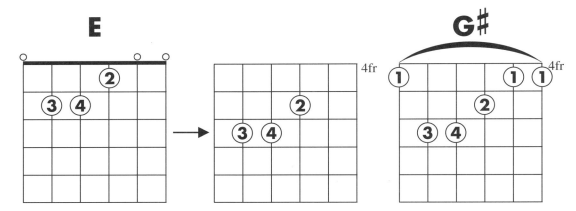

By playing the E7 chord with the new fingering, you can play other 7 chords up the neck. Try out the F♯7 and G♯7 barre chords.

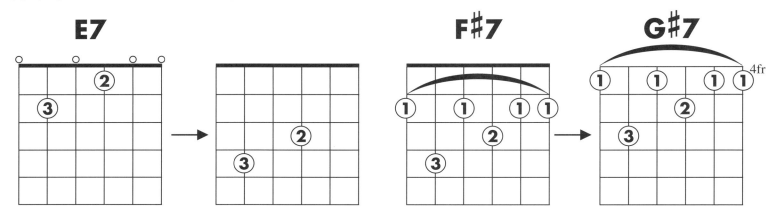

The Em chord can be moved up the neck in the same way. Now create the F♯m and G♯m barre chords.

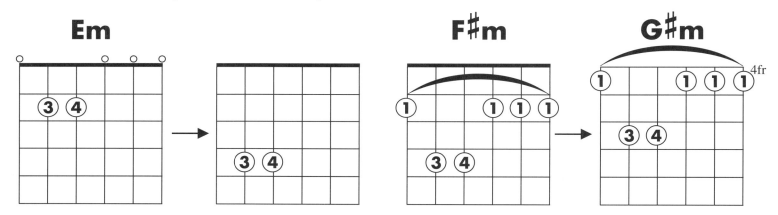

There are two other open-position chord types that can also be moved up and down the neck. Learn these fingerings for the Em7 and Emaj7 chords and apply them to the chord progressions on the next page.

Em7 = (E minor 7)

Emaj7 = (E major 7)

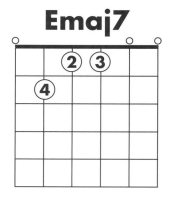

PLAYING CHORDS

Play the chord progressions below. They demonstrate how barre chords are often interspersed with open-position chords in real music. Experiment with different combinations of chords. Play barre chords only when you have to, or try playing all the progressions with barre chords (using E- and A-shape barre chords). Make sure the chord changes are smooth and you get to the new chord on time.

TRACK 48

144. CHORD WORKOUT 2

PLAYING CHORDS

The Big Four

If we refer to the chord roots of B, F♯, C♯, and G♯ as the "Big Four," you will begin to notice that these points are where a lot of barre chords appear in guitar music. Play through the chord progressions below using barre chords built off the notes on the A and E strings. Focus on moving the least amount of space possible to find the next chord, which can also be an open-position chord.

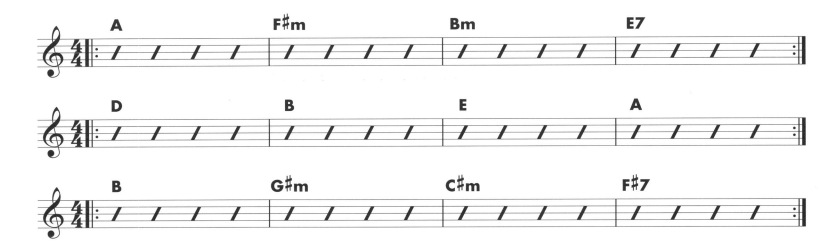

L-7 Approach

Study the diagram below. Notice how the roots for the primary chord progressions appear in an "L" or "7" shape. It might help to lay your book on its side edge to better see the shapes. This concept will also help to locate starting points for finding keys and scales all over the guitar neck. The chord progression for "Wild Thing" on page 60 makes use of the L7 approach.

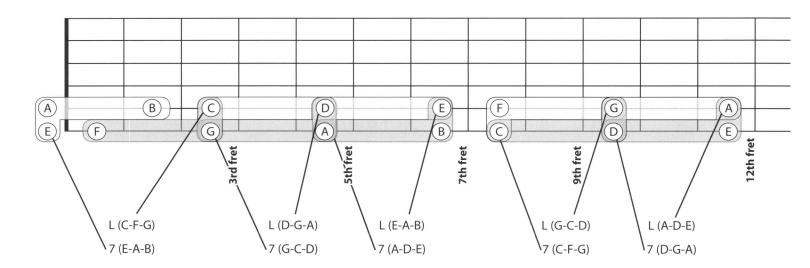

 **Alert**   Knowing the "L-7 Approach" will help you with jazz band charts and a variety of other applications.

PERFORMANCE SPOTLIGHT

"Day Tripper" is a great example of using all the roots of the "Big Four" principle. You will find them (F♯, G♯, C♯, B) in the chorus of this classic Beatles song. Alternate between picking the main riff (the intro and outro notes) and strumming the chords. Strum pattern 3 works well for this song. You should also try picking the melody line.

TRACK 49

145. DAY TRIPPER

Words and Music by John Lennon
and Paul McCartney

NEW RHYTHMS

THEORY

A **sixteenth note** receives one-fourth of a beat, and therefore it takes four of them to equal a single quarter note. Likewise, two sixteenth notes equal the value of one eighth note. The sixteenth-note stem has two flags when played alone or two beams when joined together with other notes.

Play through this chart to get an idea of how these notes are subdivided into the other rhythms.

4 Quarter Notes =

8 Eighth Notes =

16 Sixteenth Notes =

THEORY

2/4 Time $\frac{2}{4}$ The following tunes are written in the **2/4 time** signature. There are two beats per measure and a quarter note gets one beat.

Play through the following tunes that feature sixteenth notes and 2/4 meter. Use alternate picking for sixteenth notes just like you do with eighth notes.

TRACK 50

146. SAILOR'S HORNPIPE

Sea Chantey

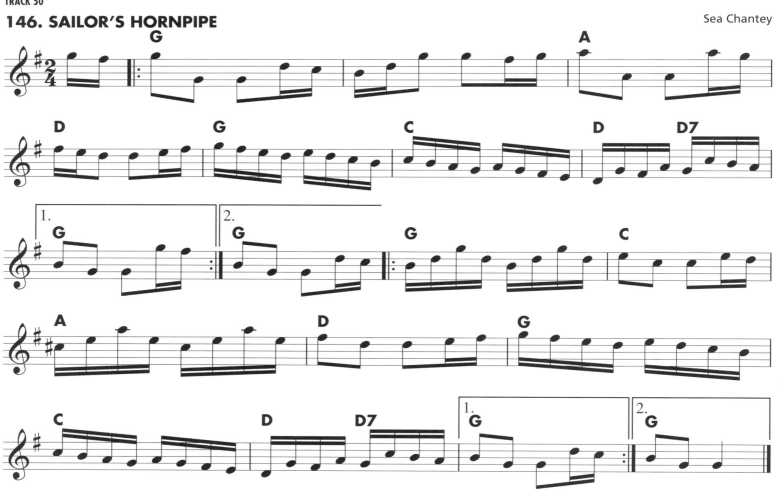

NEW RHYTHMS

TRACK 51

147. DEVIL'S DREAM

Traditional Fiddle Tune

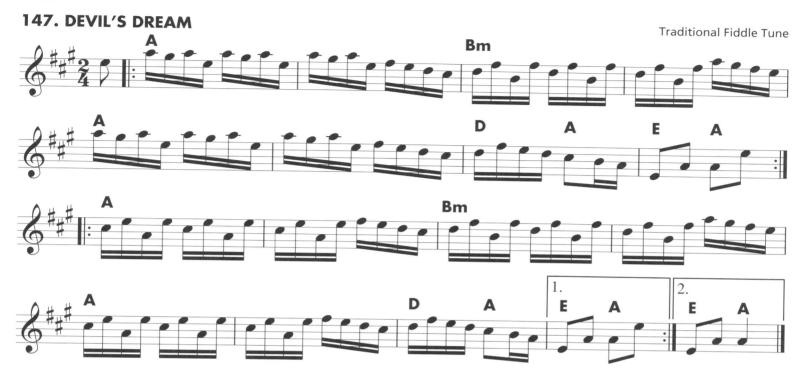

Dotted Eighth Note

A **dotted eighth note** works in the same way as other dotted notes you've learned. Since an eighth note gets half a beat and the dot receives half of that, you end up with 3/4 of a beat. Often a sixteenth note is added to complete the full beat.

THEORY

$$\frac{4}{4} \quad \frac{3}{4} \quad \frac{2}{4} \qquad \flat \; + \; \cdot \; = \; \flat\!\cdot \; + \; \flat \; = \; \flat\!\cdot\!\flat$$

½ beat   ¼ beat   ¾ beat   ¼ beat   1 beat

TRACK 52

148. TWINKLE, TWINKLE LITTLE STAR *Play this familiar tune that features the new dotted eighth and sixteenth note combination.*

Traditional

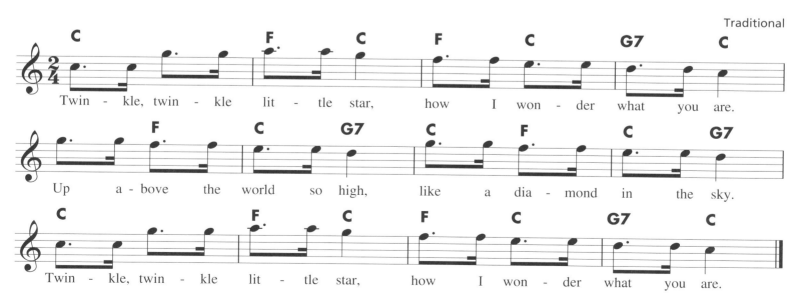

Twin - kle, twin - kle lit - tle star, how I won - der what you are.

Up a - bove the world so high, like a dia - mond in the sky.

Twin - kle, twin - kle lit - tle star, how I won - der what you are.

PLAYING POSTIONS

In order to play higher notes on the staff, you have to play higher in pitch up the fretboard. Let's look at two related scales you studied earlier in the book—C major and A minor—and play them at the 5th fret, or fifth position.

Study the letter names below in the scale diagram, and then play the following exercises in the fifth position. Play them slowly until you can find all the notes and then work them up to speed.

- Index finger plays notes at the 5th fret.
- Middle finger plays notes at the 6th fret.
- Ring finger plays notes at the 7th fret.
- Pinky finger plays notes at the 8th fret.
- B on the 3rd string is played with index finger.

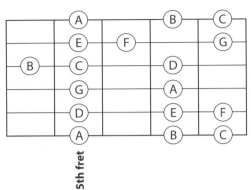

149. CROSSING OVER THE C

150. THIRD TIME'S A CHARM

TRACK 53

151. TURKEY IN THE STRAW (B SECTION) *Here's the B section of this well-known tune that you played in the beginning of the book.*

American Folksong

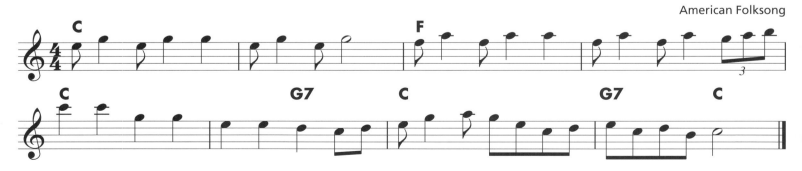

152. ESSENTIAL CREATIVITY *Now go back to page 5 and combine the A and B sections of "Turkey in the Straw." Try playing both parts in fifth position.*

PLAYING POSITIONS

The pentatonic scale is also movable, just like the barre chords and other scales you learned earlier. We are now going to move the pentatonic scale to the 5th fret and play it there.

Study the letter names below in the scale diagram, and then play the following exercises in the fifth position.

 **Alert**   The key of A minor contains the same notes as the key of C major, making them relative keys. When you start the pentatonic scale on A it is a minor pentatonic scale, and when you start it on C it is a major pentatonic scale.

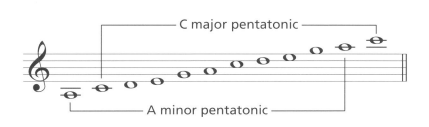

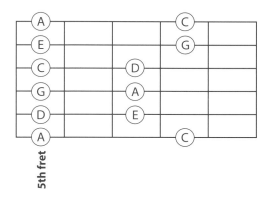

Play the scales below and focus on a strict down-up alternating picking pattern. When you stop on an A it will sound like a minor scale, and when you stop on a C it will sound major.

153. A MINOR PENTATONIC

154. C MAJOR PENTATONIC

The triplet pattern below can be found in many familiar rock songs. This one is in A minor.

155. TWO STEPS FORWARD, ONE STEP BACK

PLAYING POSITIONS

Play through the licks below that use the A minor pentatonic and C major pentatonic scales.

156. LICK 1

TRACK 54

157. LICK 2

TRACK 55

158. LICK 3

TRACK 56

159. LICK 4

TRACK 57

160. LICK 5

TRACK 58

161. LICK 6

TRACK 59

162. LICK 7

TRACK 60

163. LICK 8

TRACK 61

 164. ESSENTIAL CREATIVITY *Make up your own licks using the A minor pentatonic and C major pentatonic scales. Play your creation/solo over the two chord progressions on the next page. Remember, as long as you are playing the notes within the scale, there is no right or wrong—it's just your solo!*

PLAYING POSITIONS

Now let's use the fifth-position pentatonic scales to play some lead guitar! Review the fretboard diagrams below and follow the steps to improvise some licks over the following chord progressions.

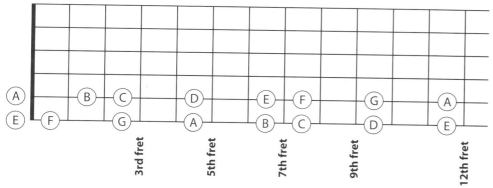
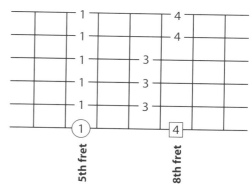

1. Try to determine the key of the song.
2. Locate that note on the 6th string.
3. Use the pentatonic scale that begins at that fret.

1   Index finger for minor keys, blues, and rock songs

4   Pinky finger for major keys, country, pop, and jazz songs

 TRACK 62

165. POWER STRUGGLER

 TRACK 63

166. ROCK-A-MY BLUES

 TRACK 64

167. MINOR INFRACTION

 TRACK 65

168. POPCORN COUNTRY

 TRACK 66

169. THE JAZZ CIRCLE

NEW TECHNIQUES

Here is a brief overview of some fun and expressive guitar techniques.

Pull-Off: Pick a fretted note and then pull your fretting finger down off the string with enough force to sound the note(s) behind it (on the same string) without picking again. In the early stages of learning this skill, it is best to fret the first note with your ring finger and pull off to the index finger. Try it out in the following exercise.

THEORY The curved line in the tablature below is called a **slur** and tells you to connect two or more notes. You will see slurs in music for a variety of techniques—most commonly for pull-offs, hammer-ons, and slides.

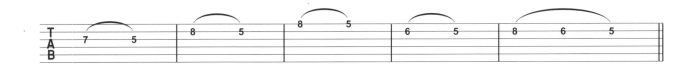

Hammer-On: This is essentially the reverse of the pull-off. Pick a note and then "hammer" a fret-hand finger down onto the fretboard for a higher note. Some force is required to ensure that the second note sounds. In the early stages of learning this skill, it is best to fret the first note with your index finger and hammer the higher note with your ring finger. Try the exercise below.

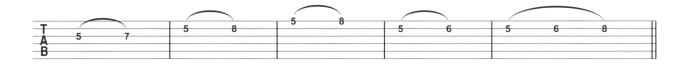

Slide: Place a fret-hand finger on a given pitch, pick that note, and then slide up or down the string to the next desired note. As you slide across the fretboard, keep enough pressure on the string so the sliding note(s) continue to sound. Play the exercise below and try the slides with different fingers.

170. ESSENTIAL CREATIVITY

Try adding these techniques to your solos. Go back to the previous section and play some licks over the given progressions using pull-offs, hammer-ons, and slides. Have fun!

NEW TECHNIQUES

Following are some well-known rock riffs you may have heard that include pull-offs, hammer-ons, and slides.

This first example is a southern rock anthem that mixes arpeggios with hammer-ons and pull-offs. Notice the new syncopated rhythm of sixteenth-eighth-sixteenth. You've already learned these note values, but here they are presented in a new combination. Take your time to learn the proper rhythmic feel.

171. SWEET HOME ALABAMA

Words and Music by Ronnie Van Zant,
Ed King and Gary Rossington

Next is a classic riff by Eric Clapton that features hammer-ons, pull-offs, and slides. Notice the sliding movable power chords. Once you've mastered this, go back to page 60 and apply the sliding power chords to the song "Iron Man."

172. LAYLA

Words and Music by Eric Clapton
and Jim Gordon

Bon Jovi's ballad "I'll Be There for You" includes this memorable intro lick performed with sliding notes on the G string.

173. I'LL BE THERE FOR YOU

Words and Music by Jon Bon Jovi
and Richie Sambora

Country superstar Brad Paisley wrote this open-string riff that features hammer-ons, pull-offs, and slides. Notice that the first note is slid into "from nowhere." Instead of starting at a specific note, you simply slide into the first note from somewhere lower on the fretboard. Also be aware of the hammer-ons that occur along with open strings—a classic country guitar technique.

174. ONLINE

Words and Music by Brad Paisley,
Chris DuBois and Kelley Lovelace

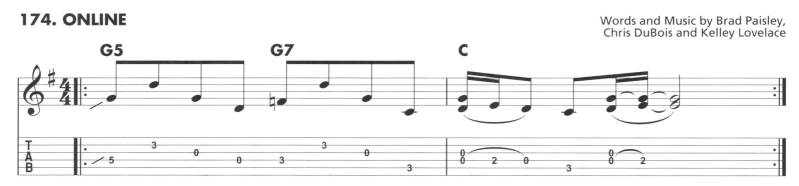

KEY OF F – NOTES

The key of F major has one flat in the key signature, B♭. The well-known chorus of "We Are the Champions" by Queen is in the key of F, and also features a new time signature called 6/8.

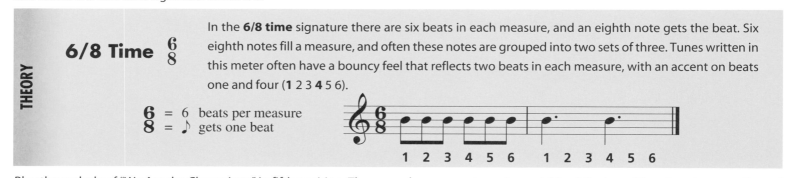

THEORY

6/8 Time $\frac{6}{8}$

In the **6/8 time** signature there are six beats in each measure, and an eighth note gets the beat. Six eighth notes fill a measure, and often these notes are grouped into two sets of three. Tunes written in this meter often have a bouncy feel that reflects two beats in each measure, with an accent on beats one and four (**1** 2 3 **4** 5 6).

$\frac{6}{8}$ = 6 beats per measure
$\frac{6}{8}$ = ♪ gets one beat

Play the melody of "We Are the Champions" in fifth position. There are also some extra notes outside of the key of F major where you'll need to shift down to fourth position to play them. Be sure to study and count through the rhythm first to get a feel for the new 6/8 time signature. Also, have a friend play along with the chords, which consist of movable power chords and barre chords.

175. WE ARE THE CHAMPIONS

Words and Music by Freddie Mercury

KEY OF Dm – NOTES

This familiar Irish fight song is also in 6/8 time. It is in the key of D minor—the relative minor of F major—so it also contains one flat in the key signature, B♭. Gtr. 2 covers the chords, while Gtr. 1 plays the melody in fifth position, but also jumps up the neck to tenth position in the B section, and eighth position in the C section. Watch the fingerings! Also notice how the chords follow the L7 approach.

176. I'M SHIPPING UP TO BOSTON

Words and Music by Alexander Barr, Ken Casey,
Woody Guthrie and Matthew Kelly

PERFORMANCE SPOTLIGHT

Work through the chords and melody of the tune below, and then put the piece together with another guitarist or as a class.

STRUM BUILDER 10

You first learned about slash chords on page 36, which are chords that contain a note other than the root in the bass. Here are some new slash chords to use in the song "King of Pain." Learn these chords before playing the tune.

- A/E is an A chord with its lowest note as an E.
- D/F♯ is a D chord with its lowest note as an F♯.
- A/G is an A chord with its lowest note as a G.
- Bm/A is a Bm chord with its lowest note as an A.

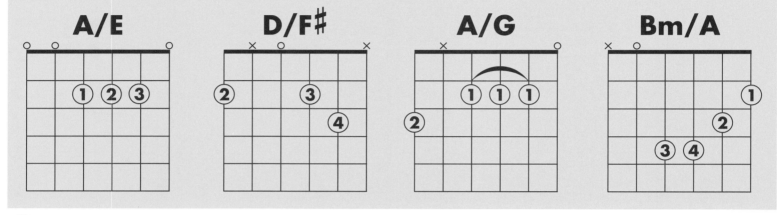

TRACK 67

177. KING OF PAIN

Music and Lyrics by Sting

CHORD CHART

Open-Position I-IV-V Chords

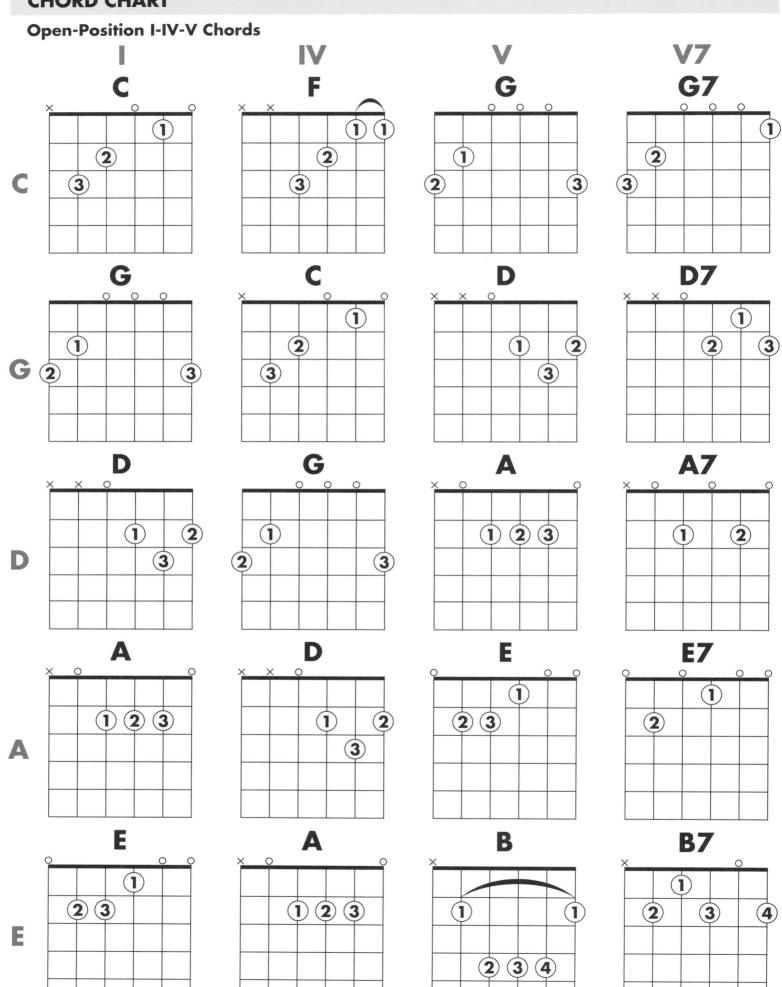

Open-Position i-iv-V Chords

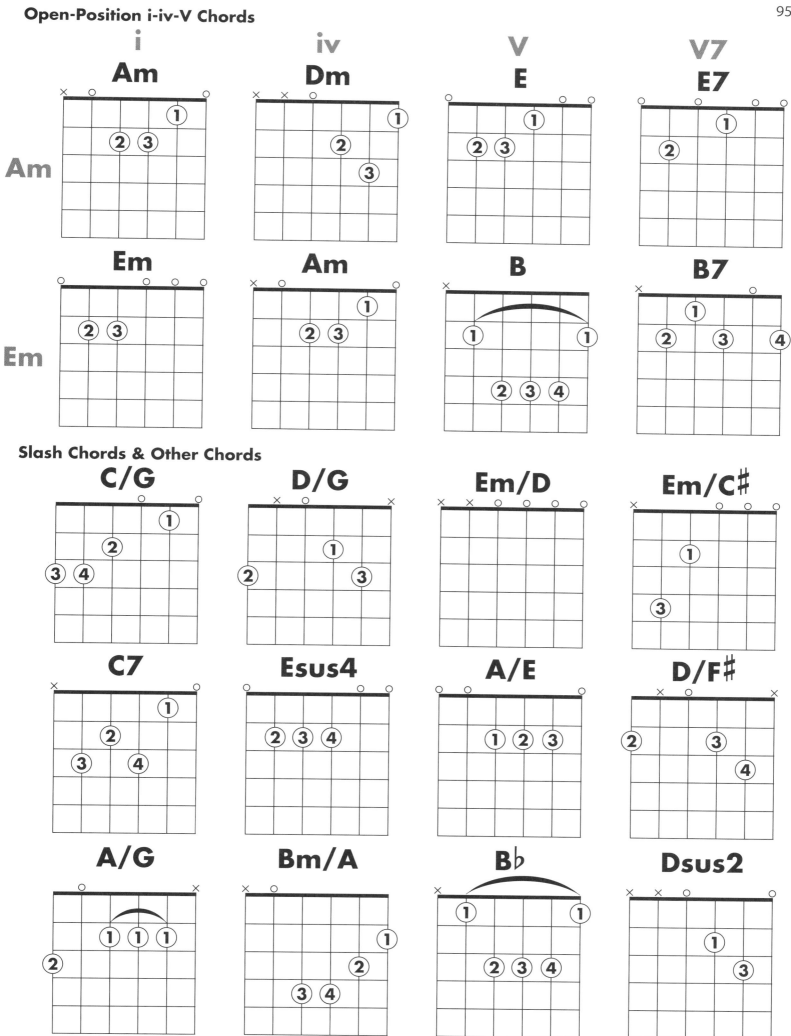

Slash Chords & Other Chords

96

 **REFERENCE INDEX**

Definitions (pg.)